Space Voyager

Sun

by Vanessa Black

Bullfrog Books

Ideas for Parents and Teachers

Bullfrog Books let children practice reading informational text at the earliest reading levels. Repetition, familiar words, and photo labels support early readers.

Before Reading

- Discuss the cover photo. What does it tell them?

- Look at the picture glossary together. Read and discuss the words.

Read the Book

- "Walk" through the book and look at the photos. Let the child ask questions. Point out the photo labels.

- Read the book to the child, or have him or her read independently.

After Reading

- Prompt the child to think more. Ask: The word "solar" means having to do with the sun. Have you heard this word before? What things can you think of that might have to do with the sun?

Bullfrog Books are published by Jump!
5357 Penn Avenue South
Minneapolis, MN 55419
www.jumplibrary.com

Library of Congress Cataloging-in-Publication Data

Names: Black, Vanessa, 1973– author.
Title: Sun / by Vanessa Black.
Description: Minneapolis, MN: Jump!, Inc., [2018]
Series: Bullfrog books. Space voyager
"Bullfrog Books are published by Jump!."
Audience: Ages 5–8. | Audience: K to grade 3.
Includes bibliographical references and index.
Identifiers: LCCN 2017021041 (print)
LCCN 2017021682 (ebook)
ISBN 9781624966910 (ebook)
ISBN 9781620318546 (hardcover: alk. paper)
ISBN 9781620318553 (pbk.)
Subjects: LCSH: Sun—Juvenile literature.
Classification: LCC QB521.5 (ebook)
LCC QB521.5 .B59 2017 (print) | DDC 523.7—dc23
LC record available at https://lccn.loc.gov/2017021041

Editor: Jenna Trnka
Book Designer: Molly Ballanger
Photo Researchers: Molly Ballanger & Jenna Trnka

Photo Credits: NASA images/Shutterstock, cover; Ilike/Shutterstock, 1; Igor Zavalskiy/Shutterstock, 3; Tom Wang/Shutterstock, 4; Elena Blokhina/Shutterstock, 5; Triff/Shutterstock, 6–7, 10; Arndt Vladimir/iStock, 8–9; Mopic/Shutterstock, 12–13, 23tl; solarseven/iStock, 14–15, 23mr; RIA Novosti/Science Source, 16–17, 23br; Johns Hopkins University Applied Physics Laboratory/NASA, 18, 23tr; Huntstock/Alamy, 19; Robert Kneschke/Shutterstock, 20–21; AlexHilv/Shutterstock, 23ml; eucyin/iStock, 23bl; Creativa Images/Shutterstock, 24.

Printed in the United States of America at Corporate Graphics in North Mankato, Minnesota.

Table of Contents

Big and Hot

The sun is hot.

It keeps us warm.

It gives us light.
It helps plants grow.

What is the sun?

It is a star.

It is made of gas.

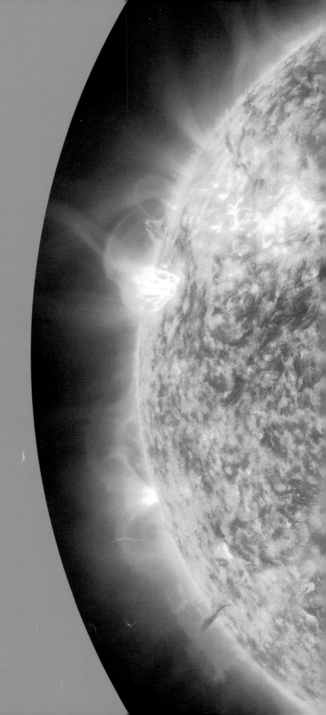

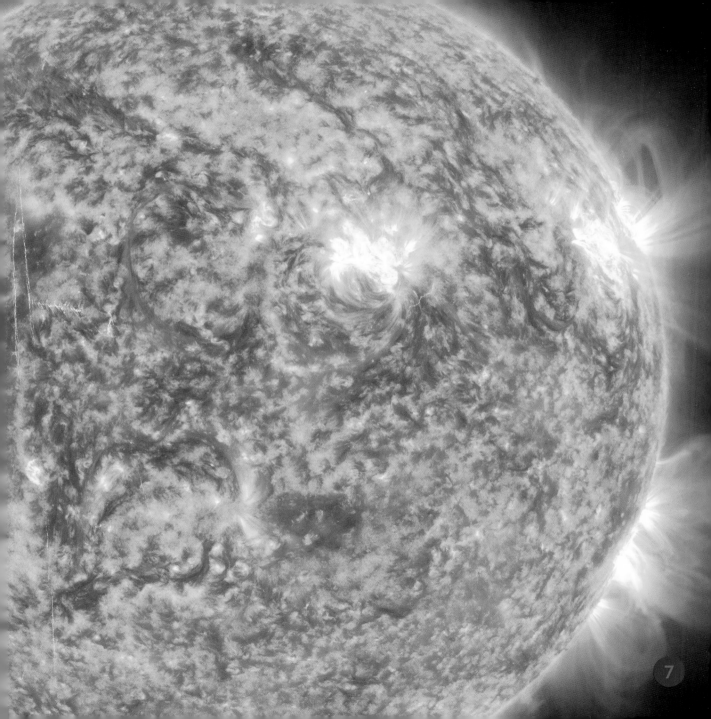

Earth

The sun is big.

One million Earths could fit inside it.

Earth orbits the sun.

Other planets do, too.

11

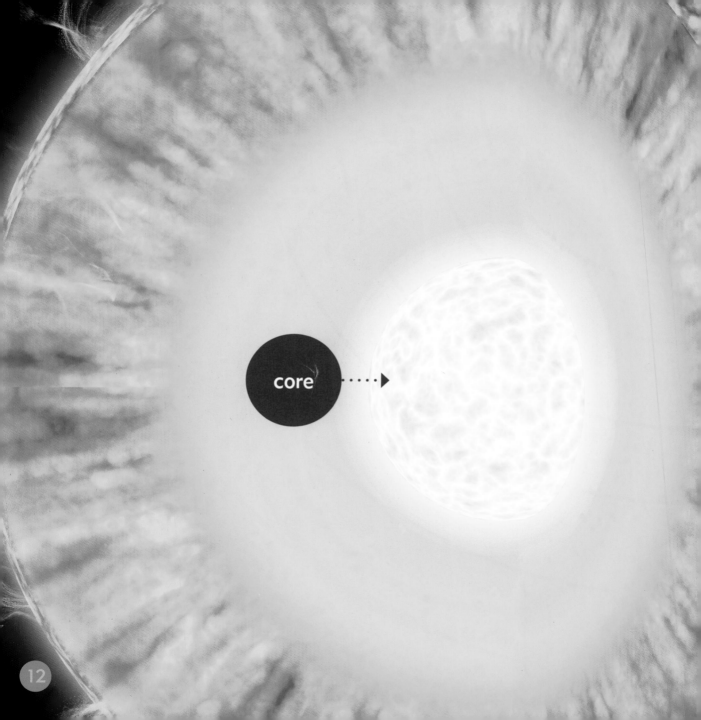

core

solar flare

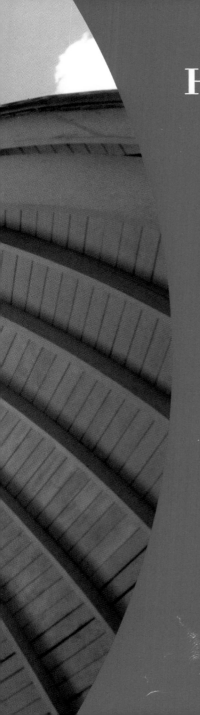

How do we know?

We use special telescopes.

We see the sun up close.

We can send
probes to the sun.
They will get close.

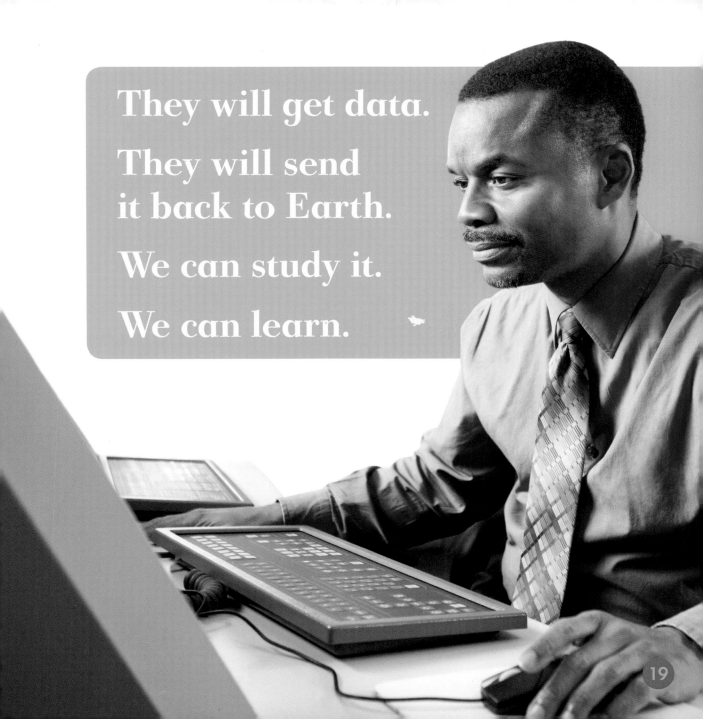

They will get data.
They will send
it back to Earth.
We can study it.
We can learn.

Wow!

Why do you like the sun?

20

A Look at the Sun

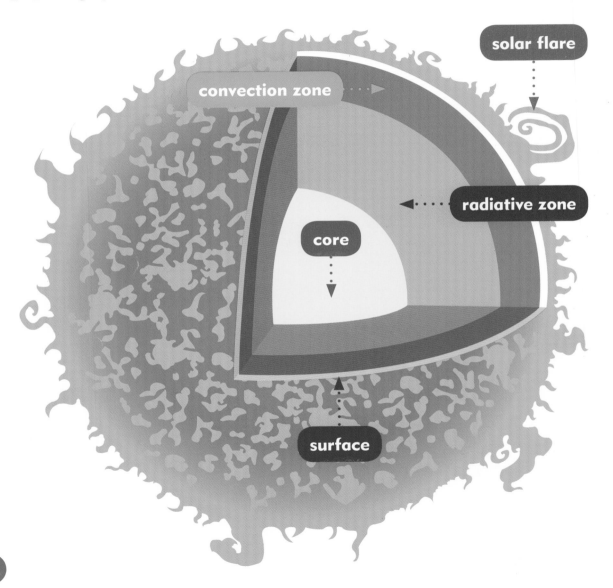

solar flare

convection zone

radiative zone

core

surface

Picture Glossary

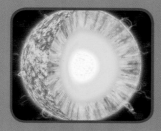
core
The inner part of the sun.

probes
Spacecraft used to explore space.

orbits
Travels around in circles.

solar flare
A sudden temporary burst of energy from a small area of the sun's surface.

planets
Large bodies that orbit the sun.

telescopes
Instruments that allow us to view distant objects.

Index

To Learn More

Learning more is as easy as 1, 2, 3.

1) Go to www.factsurfer.com

2) Enter "sun" into the search box.

3) Click the "Surf" button to see a list of websites.

With factsurfer.com, finding more information is just a click away.